FLOWER ARRANGEMENTS

FOR

SPECIAL OCCASIONS

By

JEAN B. AMER

A MARGARET HAROLD PUBLICATION

PUBLISHED BY ALLIED PUBLICATIONS, INCORPORATED

4110 HILLSBORO ROAD, NASHVILLE 12, TENN.

ACKNOWLEDGMENTS

I wish to thank my husband, Louis Amer, for his mechanical aid, the Collins West Towne Florist Shop, and Ahern's Florists for their consideration and assistance in getting special material for me, and Lewis Henderson, the photographer, who worked indefatigably to produce clear and colorful pictures. I also want to give special thanks to the following ladies for the use of their dishes, accessories, and garden material: Mrs. A. M. Walker, Mrs. Chas. McCoy, Mrs. Bob Krummel, Mrs. Jamie Cleere, Mrs. Frank Ulmer, Mrs. I. J. Spallino, Mrs. Ralph Lipps, Mrs. Frank Bowling and Mrs. Rodney Lewis. And last, but in no way least, I want to thank Margaret Harold for her patience, understanding and her delightful editing.

—Jean B. Amer

Library of Congress Catalog Card Number 62-14457

copyright, 1962
Allied Publications, Incorporated
Nashville, Tennessee

Color separations by Gulbenk Engraving Co.
Nashville, Tennessee

LITHO U.S.A. BY GIBBS-INMAN PRINTING COMPANY
LOUISVILLE, KENTUCKY

PUBLISHER'S
PREFACE

The purpose of this book is twofold. First, it is intended as a sparkling guide to garden clubbers with themes to interpret for their competitive flower shows. Here in these pages the reader will find many excellent ideas for interpretations of twenty-five different themes or special occasions. In this respect, the book is essentially one of ideas.

However, the main purpose of this book is to present artistic flower arrangements to the homemaker seeking beauty and individuality in her own party decorations . . . whatever the occasion. For this purpose, these arrangements are intended to be copied.

It is the further intention of this book to give the reader a "one-stop shop" for entertaining . . . the menu, the recipe, the decorations, and a few ideas on making her party a memorable success.

It should be pointed out that in some of the illustrations in this book, a few pieces of tableware have been placed along with the arrangement. The reader might wonder why the entire table was not set up and shown in the picture. Entire table settings were not included because they would cause the arrangement to be taken at such a distance as to lose almost all detail . . . thus making the arrangement impossible to copy. Where we have used table settings, we have not limited our use to those that appealed to us personally, but attempted to show that gracious entertainment is as possible with ordinary kitchen pottery as with fine china and sterling.

We believe that any reader who will take the time and make the effort to follow the suggestions in this book cannot help but improve her flower arranging and party-giving techniques.

—*Margaret Harold*

CONTENTS

CONTENTS

After the Concert

AN EXTREMELY popular custom that grows more popular every year is the near-midnight supper. Whatever the occasion for these late suppers, serving them strikes a note of informality. The Candlelight Cheese Cake suggested here is fluffy and light . . . not at all too heavy for the late hour. It is from Patricia Murphy's most unusual and helpful book, *Glow of Candlelight*.

MENU

Celery Stuffed with Roquefort Cheese

and White Wine

Turkey Sandwiches

Grapefruit-Avocado Salad

French Dressing

Candlelight Cheese Cake

Coffee

Candlelight Cheese Cake

1 cup graham cracker crumbs	1 pound soft cream cheese
1¼ cups sugar, divided	4 whole eggs
¾ cup soft butter	2½ cups heavy cream

Dairy sour cream

Combine crumbs, ½ cup sugar and butter; press on bottom and sides of 8-inch spring form pan. Whip cheese until fluffy; beat in remaining sugar; continue beating until light and fluffy. Add eggs, one at a time, beating well after each addition. Stir in heavy cream. Strain through sieve into pan. Bake at 325° 1 hour. Turn oven off; leave cheese cake in oven 1 hour. Remove from oven; let cool gradually to room temperature; chill. Top with layer of dairy sour cream.

DANCE OR MUSIC CLUB PARTY

Here's a graceful table decoration that will delight the guests at your
dance or music club party. Use phonograph records as your base to
establish the music theme, overlapping four of them, as shown, and
placing one upright toward the back of the arrangement for balance.
(This record can be held upright by a plate holder, which will be concealed by the records in the foreground and the flowers resting on
them.) Arrange magnolia branches and lavender gladioli in a tall and
widespread design, using a cup holder. The dancing girl on the record
base adds atmosphere, but you can use a different figure if you wish.

AFTER THE CONCERT

This clever design will recapture the spell of the concert and be the perfect conversation piece at an after-the-concert party. To make it for your own refreshment table, use a brass, footed stand for your base. Fasten a twiggy branch on it with floral clay. Then arrange branches of euonymus and gold glitter grapes in a trailing, graceful fashion as shown, allowing some of the grapes to spill out over a mat under the stand. Place two horns, one midway in the arrangement on a branch, and the other on the stand in a balanced manner as shown. As a finishing touch, make notes and staff of pipe cleaners and pin them to a plain backdrop immediately behind the arrangement . . . or secure them firmly to the ends of the tree branches with florist wire.

Fourth of July

FOR A FOURTH of July gathering that will really go over with a bang, have an old-fashioned picnic with some new-fashioned food. You can have it in your back yard or on the patio, and decorate the outdoor table simply, but effectively, with the symbols of the day. Furnish your guests with some gay paper hats and noisemakers and make your picnic a real celebration.

At any picnic, the food's the thing! And the barbecue sauce below is a recipe of Jack Lemmon's. He says it'll make *anything* taste good. Try it with the lowly hamburger for a delightful surprise.

MENU

Hamburgers with Barbecue Sauce

Vegetable Shish-Kabobs

Rolls

Iced Tea

Chilled Watermelon

Barbecue Sauce

3 cups catsup	1 whole garlic clove, minced
chili powder, or 3 chopped chili peppers	1 halved onion, medium size
	¼ cup lemon juice
1 teaspoon English mustard	1 bay leaf
1 teaspoon black pepper (freshly ground is best)	1 healthy slug of a sharp salad dressing
1 tablespoon Worcestershire sauce	¾ cup maple syrup
	¼ pound butter

Mix and bring to boil. Simmer one hour. Remove onion and bay leaf before serving hot . . . and serve it on anything!

FOURTH OF JULY

In a tall, white vase, arrange (fan-like) several long, red-and-white paper straws or slender peppermint candy sticks. Use a needle-point holder, fastened onto the top of the container, to hold them. Now, add a small amount of juniper low in the design for depth and as background for tiny silk flags. Then, to give your design a rich look, drape blue satin ribbon through the handles of the vase, and bring it down softly around the white alabaster base. For balance and added eye interest, attach more small flags to the ribbon at the sides of the vase.

FOURTH OF JULY

This exciting effect is achieved through the use of contrast in color and of swift modern lines. To create this design, use an ultra-modern black vase with openings at both top and bottom. Then arrange white gladioli and red geraniums in a graceful upward sweep, as shown, in both top and bottom of container, using tips of blue juniper for both texture and additional color. For maximum effectiveness, place the arrangement on a white glass tile . . . with small flags displayed on either side.

Showers

SHOWERS are a happy custom . . . always in season . . . and never restricted as to time. Your shower can be in the form of a luncheon, an afternoon tea, a buffet supper, or an after-dinner party with light refreshments. The Lemon Bibbit has been chosen as the dessert because of its versatility. It would go equally well at a buffet supper or an afternoon tea. It is Nelson Riddle's recipe . . . and according to him, it's a masterpiece. As he put it, "This dessert is as fragile as good jazz . . . and just as exciting." The rest of your menu would, of course, be governed by the hour of your party.

LUNCHEON MENU

Chopped Chicken Livers on Lettuce

Oysters on Half Shell

Broccoli Polonaise

Hot Rolls

Lemon Bibbit

Coffee

Lemon Bibbit

1 can condensed milk	Grated rind of 1 lemon
1 cup sugar	¼ cup lemon juice
1 pkg. lemon jello	¾ cup boiling water

1 pkg. vanilla wafers

Chill one can (1-2/3 cups) condensed milk, to whip. Mix together 1 cup sugar, 1 pkg. lemon jello, grated rind of one lemon, a generous ¼ cup lemon juice, and ¾ cup boiling water. Stir until jello is dissolved. Chill until slightly firmed. Whip condensed milk; fold into jello. Into buttered casserole, lined with 1 pkg. crushed vanilla wafers, pour lemon mixture. Top with leftover wafer crumbs. Chill thoroughly to set before serving.

BABY SHOWER

This unique arrangement for tea table at a baby shower shows just how much can be accomplished with very little material. A large, pink, glass tray is an excellent container for an offside arrangement of lenten rose leaves and pink roses. First, place the leaves as shown, using a large cup holder to keep the material fresh. Then place roses with stems of varying lengths . . . using a large rose at the leaf center to heighten the effect. The stork here was originally a cracker basket, but a paper stork could be used, too. As an added touch, and to balance the entire arrangement, use small packages grouped at one end of the tray.

KITCHEN SHOWER

This eye-catching and colorful design is a perfect decoration for a kitchen shower. First, select a bright, shiny dust pan (the one here is copper-colored). Set it upright as shown. Then wedge a large lump of floral clay inside the pan to secure the stems of the materials. Arrange branches of artificial Scotch broom (sprayed copper) to form a line, with copper foil leaves and artificial lady apples. Attach thin wires to the apples and leaves so that they'll be easy to secure at an attractive angle. Copper-colored measuring cups placed at the lower left add unity and balance, in addition to contributing interest.

SHOWER

This gay umbrella door piece is perfect for any type of shower, and it's easy to make, too. First, spray a basket umbrella with silver paint. Then tape beautiful packages from top to bottom, and add a large bow at the top. The arrangement may be secured to the door by means of wire at the back of the design. Or, if preferred, you may place it indoors by using a wire stand or anything else strong enough to support the design without detracting from the effectiveness.

KITCHEN SHOWER

Any new bride is sure to develop a nodding acquaintance with the potato . . . and what could be more effective than this "potato" tree decoration for that kitchen shower in her honor! Begin with a wooden Lazy Susan or something similar as your container. To its wooden base, fasten a twiggy, sturdy branch. The one shown here is a manzanita branch. Next, scrub and wax several potatoes of comparatively uniform size, and wedge them onto the branches, leaving several to be grouped amid the foliage at the base of the branch. Several different kinds of foliage would serve, but the one used here is andromeda . . . because it stays fresh for a long time, even out of water.

SHOWER

A rare combination of delicacy and elegance is achieved in this design . . . through strict adherence to color scheme and the use of unadorned container and base. To duplicate this arrangement for a shower, first wedge a paper umbrella onto the rim of a white vase with floral clay. Then arrange blue delphinium, white snapdragons, and pink roses in a horizontal fashion under the parasol. Now place small packages beneath the arrangement for added balance and eye interest.

Weddings and Anniversaries

WHILE WEDDING RECEPTIONS demand a certain formality in both decoration and table arrangement, anniversaries can be delightful little informal gatherings. However, both are worthy of the ultimate in the decorating as well as the preparation and serving of food. If there is to be a cocktail party for the guest of honor, the sauerkraut balls below would make excellent companions to cocktails or appetizers. They were created for and are presently served in Patricia Murphy's Candlelight Restaurants in Westchester and Fort Lauderdale.

Sauerkraut Balls

2 large onions, finely chopped	2 cups flour
1 bunch celery, finely chopped	½ teaspoon salt
3 tablespoons butter	½ teaspoon Ac'cent
1 pound ground lean beef	⅛ teaspoon pepper
2 cups well-drained sauerkraut	2 eggs

Cook onion and celery in butter until brown. Add beef; cook over low heat about 8 minutes. Cool. Add sauerkraut (this must be very dry), flour, seasonings and unbeaten eggs. Mix thoroughly. Shape into balls 1-inch in diameter. Fry in deep fat heated to 390° about 2 minutes or until brown. Drain on absorbent paper. Serve hot. Makes 20 to 25 servings.

WEDDINGS AND ANNIVERSARIES

This elaborate and perfectly proportioned design will go to the head of any guest of honor. To make it for your favorite honoree's table at an announcement, shower or anniversary, first place a candle tree on a basket tray. The tree will lend support for candles and flowers alike, in addition to establishing the mood of the piece. When your container is placed, tuck short-stemmed white and yellow mums and arborvitae around the candles. Then make individual corsages of greens, mums, and small natural apples, tying them with green ribbon bows. Place these carefully in a circular manner on the basket tray at the base of the candle tree. Be careful to place them in keeping with the uncluttered appearance of the overall arrangement.

WEDDINGS AND ANNIVERSARIES

When wedding bells ring, this delicate arrangement is perfect for the table at the reception. To duplicate it, begin with a wire brass bell as a container. Make a fan-shaped arrangement of pink and white carnations inside the bell, using a cup holder to keep them fresh, and letting them spread gently downward as shown. Using another cup holder below the bell, make a similar fan-shaped arrangement of short-stemmed carnations. Elevate the arrangement by placing the bell on a flower pot holder, which is concealed by the lower carnations. The ribbon bow at the top of the bell is in keeping with the color scheme.

20

WEDDINGS AND ANNIVERSARIES

To celebrate the golden wedding anniversary, no arrangement could
be more appropriate than this design in tones of gold. An old brass
lamp base, such as the one shown, is the ideal container for this tablepiece, but a similar container would be just as effective. Begin by
arranging large majestic lilies and framing them with yellow snapdragons and yellow honeysuckle branches. Be careful to keep the
flowers low so that the arrangement is below eye level. Now add gold
glitter grapes for distinction . . . and complete the gold theme by
placing the finished design on a gold mat.

WEDDINGS AND ANNIVERSARIES

Paper means a wedding anniversary, the very first one . . . and paper, indeed, plays an important part in this unusual arrangement. To reconstruct this design for your own table, begin with a flat bowl and needle-point holder. Arrange branches of Japanese holly so that they form a triangle as shown and also form a background for the trimming. Make branch trimmings by bunching together small lace doilies with tiny yellow and bronze strawflowers wired in the center. Use a green candle in a glass candle holder to provide added interest and balance; as a final touch, make a collar of paper doilies for the candle. Your accessories? Paper, of course!

WEDDINGS AND ANNIVERSARIES

Here's a refreshing version of the ball and chain . . . a perfect centerpiece for the bachelor's last fling! To make this gently humorous and
highly effective design, start with a black and silver cloth as a base and
a black glass cake stand as a container. Spray a large styrofoam ball
with silver paint, and place it directly in the center of the container as
the focal point of the entire design. Place silvered baptisia pods and
treated black magnolia leaves fan-like around the ball, wedging them
into the styrofoam. Curve a natural-colored chain, sprayed with silver
paint, down and around black-and-white glasses. The one lone glass on
the right completes your design on an interesting note.

WEDDINGS AND ANNIVERSARIES

This enchanting arrangement will brighten the dinner table at any anniversary party . . . from the first to the 50th. Using a three-candle candelabrum with pink, twist candles, arrange gold and pink glitter grapes and pink rose buds with leaves. Then tape them all around the candle as shown. Lay clusters of grapes on the gold mat below, and your vision in pink and gold is complete. Though all the materials used here are artificial, you may wish to tuck in a few fresh greens just moments before the guests arrive.

WEDDINGS AND ANNIVERSARIES

Roses and silver give eloquent expression to a silver wedding anniversary table. To make this delicately composed arrangement, begin with a high but not tall silver container. The container here was improvised from a large silver serving dish placed atop a silver candy dish. Arrange pink roses with blue delphinium and white snapdragons with a touch of purple statice as shown, being careful to keep your arrangement high so that it will not interfere with other items which must be on the table. Accessories should be in keeping with this delicate color scheme, as are the pink damask cloth and tapestry rose bone china dishes here.

WEDDINGS AND ANNIVERSARIES

The candelabrum is never more at home than at a wedding or anniversary party. Here, the traditional white . . . symbolic of weddings and anniversaries . . . is used with a silver candelabrum to produce a striking effect. To duplicate this arrangement, begin with white gladioli, breaking them to the desired height, and arranging them in a jello mold with water and needle holder. Place them in front of the candelabrum, so that they appear to cling gently to the middle candle. (The candles used here are also white.) For color, place sprays of artificial, green, cherry-tomatoes or other small fruit through the center.

Father's Day

HERE'S AN idea for a Father's Day celebration . . . or for any adult birthday . . . whether you plan a breakfast, luncheon, dinner or buffet supper. It is Bing Crosby's favorite recipe . . . Turkey and Eggs a la Crosby. He says, "It's the greatest. A breeze to toss together . . . a vision when it's served." The menu below is just a suggestion. Naturally, you will want to serve the honoree's favorite foods, if possible.

MENU for a BUFFET

Caesar Salad

Turkey and Eggs a la Crosby

Green Peas

Hot Rolls

Cake with Candles

Ice Cream

Coffee

Turkey and Eggs a la Crosby

For each serving: Place two slices of turkey in buttered baking dish; on top, break two eggs. Sprinkle one teaspoon diced onions over top, salt and pepper as you like it. Add one-half cup cream. Bake in slow oven, 300 degrees, 20 minutes. Serve on hot buttered toast.

FATHER'S DAY OR BIRTHDAY

You'll give Dad a new lease on life with this arrangement designed especially for his birthday and placed in his favorite nook. Use a large, polished burl for the base and a colorful stein as a container for an arrangement of his favorite flowers. Used here are deep red daisy mums with yellow centers and yellow snapdragons. A masculine grouping of gifts . . . a book, a card, and cigars, fancifully tied . . . add to the charm of the arrangement. Individual cakes, each with its own tiny candle, will bring a smile of pleasure.

BIRTHDAY CELEBRATION

Here's something fluffy, dainty, and elegant for a birthday celebration. To duplicate this colorful design for your own celebrant, begin with a raised basket container. The one shown here is bronze, but one of another type would be just as effective. Place a cup holder with water inside the basket, and arrange yellow carnations and purple statice as shown, so that the yellow in the arrangement is predominant. Place the birthday cake on a pedestal beside the basket arrangement, being sure to use candles which repeat the yellow and purple of the flowers. As a finishing touch, place one well-shaped carnation and several purple statice blooms in the center of the birthday cake. The gift of jewelry has purposely been left unwrapped to add sparkle.

Mother's Day

MOTHER'S DAY calls for a tea . . . a delightful way to show love and respect, and to give Mother an opportunity to enjoy her own friends. Delicacy and beauty should be the keynotes of decorations and refreshments alike. Arrangements of her favorite flowers . . . either as a centerpiece or as an attractive addition to the living room or hall, will be sure to please her and to catch the eyes of all your guests. As an added touch to your tea, fashion a small corsage for each mother.

MENU

Assorted Tea Sandwiches

Blueberry Nut Rounds

Brownies with Whipped Cream

Tea

Blueberry Nut Rounds

Heat oven to 375° (quick moderate). Take one package of Blueberry Muffin Mix. (Betty Crocker's are used here.) Make muffins as directed on package . . . except add ½ cup chopped nuts before folding in blueberries. Pour into three 10½ oz. soup cans or five 6-oz. frozen juice concentrate cans which have been greased just on the inside bottom of the can. *Bake 40 to 45 minutes.* Cool slightly; ease out with spatula. Slice when cool and spread with butter or softened cream cheese.

MOTHER'S DAY

To make this special arrangement for Mother's Day, begin with a heavy glass goblet sprayed with copper or gold. Next, tie a house plant (the variegated pothos plant is a good choice) to a piece of bark or a small piece of driftwood. Make a corsage of yellow roses, brown fronds, and brown and gold ribbon to nestle in the goblet as shown, and another using the same materials, to rest on the mirror base. The crystal necklace gift makes an eye-catching accessory to the arrangement.

MOTHER'S DAY

Roses are for Mother's Day! To make this exquisite table piece for her day, arrange pink roses, red violet prunus foliage and pink astilbe blooms in a silver fruit bowl with cup holder. This arrangement is pleasing for dinner guests seated all around the table, making conversation easy. A cup holder with water keeps the flowers fresh. Use china with a pink rose design, or plain china with a touch of pink coloring for added eye interest and balance.

Garden Club

PERHAPS no group presents quite the challenge to a hostess as her own garden club. A luncheon for these colleagues, however, can be a delightful occasion and one that will be remembered for months. You should arrange your own specialty as attractively as possible . . . whether it be gladioli, dahlias, azaleas . . . or roses. A simple and appropriate arrangement can catch and becalm the most critical eye. For dessert, we suggest the Viennese Velvet. It is so easy to make that you'll have to taste it to believe how downright superb it really is. But if you'll be sure that the ice cream you use is first-rate and the coffee freshly brewed, we'll guarantee that it'll "bring the house down."

MENU

Honey Dew, Watermelon and Cantaloupe Balls
in White Wine

Baked Asparagus and Tomato Slices with Cheddar Cheese Topping

Hot Rolls

Viennese Velvet

Coffee

Viennese Velvet

1 quart vanilla ice cream   6 cups hot, double-strength coffee

Whipped Cream

Place one large scoop of vanilla ice cream in each of six tall glasses. Pour hot, double-strength coffee carefully over ice cream until glass is about 2/3 full. Add a second scoop of ice cream and fill glass with coffee. Garnish with whipped cream, and add a sprinkle of nutmeg if desired. You will need long spoons for the first half of this dessert-beverage, but you will drink the latter half.

GARDEN CLUB

Simplicity is the word for this arrangement, designed to impress fellow arrangers at the garden club party. To accomplish the clean, swift lines of modern design evident here, begin with a modern gray compote vase on a black stand. Place ti leaves as a background for several blossoms of sarracenia (or similar blossoms if these are unavailable). Conceal the mechanics of the arrangement by filling in gray stones at the mouth of the container. For dramatic effect, this arrangement is best placed on a mantel or plain table.

GARDEN CLUB

Simplicity is often the secret of elegance. To make this effective center-piece for your garden club party, select a silver container like this ancient coffee server . . . or a more modern one, if you choose. Arrange silvered mahonia and carnations so that the eye is led first to the center of the arrangement and then gracefully upward. The addition of silver glass grapes adds contrast and a touch of elegance, while other silver items on the table coordinate the total.

GARDEN CLUB

The delicate grace of this design is achieved through its careful composition. Begin with a strong, beautiful branch imbedded in a wooden container and placed on a rustic plaque. Then follow the lines of the branch with tips of Scotch pine, as shown, placing them in a cup holder behind the branch and allowing some of them to sweep gently forward, concealing the container. The feathered birds and the ceramic figure of St. Francis complete the scene. The lighted candle is optional.

Buffet Supper

ENTERTAINING should be as much fun for the hostess as it is for the guests. Of course, giving parties with ease depends on many things, but most of all it means using menus and preparing foods you can count on to be successful . . . as well as doing all possible work in advance. To further guarantee the success of your party, plan it around some special occasion . . . and let your food and decorations carry out the theme. The Diamond Chicken Liver Pâté is from Patricia Murphy's book, *Glow of Candlelight*.

MENU
Diamond Chicken Liver Pâté
Assorted Crackers
Congealed Salad
Meat Balls in Chafing Dish
Hot Noodles
Spinach with Crisp Bacon Crumbs
Hot Rolls
Pineapple Upside Down Cake
Coffee

Diamond Liver Pâté

1 small onion, minced	½ teaspoon salt
1 pound butter, divided	⅛ teaspoon white pepper
1 pound fresh chicken livers, diced	or Tabasco
	1 clove garlic, minced
1½ cups clear chicken broth, divided	⅓ cup cognac
	1 cup roasted walnuts, chopped
4 tablespoons Marsala wine	
½ teaspoon paprika	1 envelope unflavored
⅛ teaspoon allspice	gelatine

Sauté onion in ½ pound butter until tender. Add diced chicken livers; cook for 10 minutes, stirring occasionally. Add half the chicken broth, Marsala wine, paprika, allspice, salt, pepper and garlic. Cook five minutes more. Place mixture in electric blender. Gradually add remaining butter (melted) and cognac. Blend until smooth. Stir in walnuts. In saucepan, sprinkle gelatine over rest of broth. Heat; stir until gelatine is dissolved. Pour part of gelatine broth into 6-cup mold. Chill for 10 minutes. Fill mold with chicken liver mixture; top with remaining broth. Keep in refrigerator for at least 6 hours before unmolding and serving.

HAWAIIAN LUAU

This colorful bit of Hawaii on your table will set the perfect stage for a luau. To make it, begin with a sturdy, low, palm leaf basket as your container. Next, place a dish of water with a needle holder toward the back of the basket. In this, arrange bright red gladioli and fresh palm branches, as shown. For a real Hawaiian look, group fruit (bananas, grapes, pomegranates) smoothly from right to left, using a fresh Hawaiian pineapple as your center of interest. To further the theme, make a lei of yellow paper, encircle the arrangement with it, and lay glad blossoms at intervals in a circular fashion to provide unity.

GEORGE WASHINGTON'S BIRTHDAY

Here's a simple but effective arrangement of a cherry tree and a hatchet to brighten your hall table in commemoration of George Washington's birthday. Begin with a strong container; the one used here is bronze, but one of pottery or wood could also be used effectively. Wedge a large lump of floral clay into the mouth of the container, and secure your "tree," which is a brown manzanita branch. Then fasten artificial cherries to the twigs of the branch with wires, and place clumps of cherries near the top of the container as shown. Lastly, add a few sprigs of artificial foliage for depth.

FOR THE BOWLERS

This modern design has a touch of realism that will intrigue the lady bowlers when they come to luncheon or supper. Using a round of white styrofoam as a base, put a large pin in an off-center position and a bowling ball just off the base. Spray both pin and ball with silver or "snow" to soften the overall effect. Next, take a small cup of water with holder, and arrange pale yellow daisy mums in a cluster with aspidistra leaves . . . allowing both mums and leaves to sweep gently downward over the base. Tiny pins with mums are given as favors. Dishes are black and white. The cloth is yellow.

FOR THE HORSY SET

Horse show enthusiasts will love this graceful and distinctive design, and the dramatic quality here will appeal to all your guests who drop in after the show or race. The striking effect is achieved through a skillful choice of setting and materials. First, place a bronze vase on a large polished burl. Then, for needed height, use a brown, twiggy branch, and place cecropia leaves and cone flowers directly under the branch. One leaf and flower below the design will dramatize the gold cup trophies and the winning ribbon. You construct the small fence simply by nailing a few pieces of wood together. It and the dignified ceramic horse emphasize the motif.

41

BUFFET SUPPER

The warm tones of this rustic design will literally enchant guests at your next buffet supper. To create it for your own table, choose a lovely piece of sculptured driftwood as your starting point. Then place the driftwood on a bamboo mat, as shown. In a cup holder behind the driftwood, arrange umbellatum lilies and the flowers and foliage of the sourwood tree, following the curve of the sculptured wood, so that the entire design becomes an "L." The strong accent on color and the adherence to simple lines make this design a dramatic one in itself, though shells may be added to heighten the effectiveness of the lilies.

NEW YEAR'S EVE

This gay and colorful design will welcome the New Year no matter where you place it, but it's a perfect arrangement for that midnight refreshment table. To copy it, begin with a silver stand as your container. Then arrange in a graceful curve leucothoe branches which have been lightly sprayed with silver paint. Secure these and small balloons wired to sticks in the container as shown. For balance, and to further the New Year's theme, make a distinctive candle holder of a wine bottle sprayed with silver and sprinkled with glue and sparkle. This makes an attractive holder for a slim candle. Add a silver bow to your candle holder, and place noisemakers and hats to complete the design.

MAY DAY TEA

This exciting maypole . . . with its charming participants . . . will bring a touch of Spring to your table. A long-stemmed goblet turned upside down magically becomes a pole for the colorful streamers, which are fastened with Scotch tape at both top and bottom. In a cup holder on top of the goblet, arrange daisies and ivy leaves as shown. Complete your arrangement by making a daisy chain to encircle the goblet and placing dolls in proper position. The dolls used here represent several nations, but other small dolls could be used just as effectively. They are fastened to the base (a glass tray) with floral clay. Since the daisy chain at the base is out of water, it will last for only one day.

Thanksgiving

THE TRADITIONAL Thanksgiving feast means abundance . . . an abundance of turkey and all the trimmin's. And since this is one meal that should be lingered over for a long time, there should be many courses . . . all favorite foods . . . that have a Thanksgiving look and a Thanksgiving taste. I assume you need no help in planning a menu of your favorite foods, but permit me a few suggestions: Whether your Thanksgiving feast is to be a breakfast for 200 or dinner en famille, the popovers below will add a festive and exciting touch. The recipe for this fluffy delicacy is the one used for Patricia Murphy's famous popovers . . . which are served in her Westchester and Fort Lauderdale Candlelight Restaurants. The sweet potato-almond pie . . . with fragrant coffee . . . will be a perfect ending for your meal.

Popovers

1 cup sifted, enriched flour	2 eggs
½ teaspoon salt	1 cup milk
1 tablespoon melted butter	

Mix and sift flour and salt. Beat eggs until light; add milk and melted butter; mix well. Sift in flour; beat until smooth. Grease popover cups or custard cups thoroughly; set in 375° oven for 5 minutes. Fill hot cups ⅓ full of batter. Bake at 375° for 50 minutes. Remove from oven; quickly cut a slit in side of each popover to allow steam to escape. Return to oven for 10 minutes. Remove popovers from cups at once to prevent them from steaming and softening. Makes 12 medium or 8 large popovers.

Sweet Potato Almond Pie

1½ cups mashed sweet potatoes	few grains salt
3 tablespoons melted butter or margarine	1 teaspoon cinnamon
	dash mace
½ cup brown sugar, firmly packed	⅓ cup chopped, toasted almonds
	1½ cups milk
3 eggs, separated	10-inch unbaked pie shell

Combine sweet potatoes, butter or margarine and brown sugar. Beat egg yolks and add. Add salt, cinnamon and mace, and mix thoroughly. Add almonds with milk to first mixture. Beat egg whites stiff and fold in. Pour into unbaked pie shell. Bake in hot oven, 425°F., 15 minutes. Reduce heat to moderately hot, 375°F. Bake 25 minutes longer, or until firm. Cool. Top with whipped cream and additional almonds.

THANKSGIVING

This clever house-and-hen centerpiece will have your guests clucking all through Thanksgiving brunch. Use a bamboo planter, shaped like a little house, as a beginning for the design. In a cup holder inside the planter, arrange red geraniums, branches of Japanese maple, long, colorful peppers, and miniature tomatoes, as shown. The gay ceramic rooster adds a colorful touch and carries out the Thanksgiving motif.

THANKSGIVING

Traditional materials and modern design result in this attractive door or wall decoration for Thanksgiving. To make it, first spray a woven mat with copper paint to use as your background . . . or leave it natural, as shown. Then fashion a line design of traditional fruits, securing them to the woven mat with wire. Be sure that the fruits you select are in good scale. The ones used here are peppers, lady apples, a peach, a large apple, and clusters of glass grapes. Arrange them as shown, giving regard to proportion and size. Next, give your design an elegant touch with a copper-colored or red shiny ribbon bow at top and bottom. Now it's ready to hang securely on a nail or hook.

THANKSGIVING

This colorful, paper turkey is the basis for an eye-catching design for the family room or den at Thanksgiving. To make this decoration, begin with two large fungi . . . one placed flat, the other upright as shown. Arrange over the fungi tiny decorative fresh pineapples, cones, artificial green grapes, and hen-and-chicks. The paper turkey is suspended from the ceiling by means of wire and wide ribbon so that it appears to be an actual part of the arrangement. If desired, this design could be used with candles instead of a turkey.

THANKSGIVING

Traditional harvest tones of gold and brown dominate this graceful Thanksgiving centerpiece. To create it for your own table, place a small pumpkin on a paper plate holder and then elevate it on a small brass stand, as shown. Then place wheat, bittersweet berries, small straw flowers, tiny fresh peppers, lady apples, and a few grapes around the pumpkin . . . being careful to avoid a cluttered appearance. Next, add some brown (treated) leather leaf fern for depth and relief. Lastly, place a cluster of fruit at the base as a transitional element. The arrangement rests on a straw mat.

THANKSGIVING

The fresh, graceful lines of this design would be excellent on the
Thanksgiving breakfast table. To copy it, begin with a bamboo mat,
which makes an excellent holder. Arrange rhododendron foliage and
dried okra pods as shown, blending in harmony with small fresh
oranges and dried sass flower. A small cup holder with water is concealed beneath the leaves to keep foliage fresh. The thoughtful ceramic
turkey repeats 'the colors in the materials and emphasizes the theme.

THANKSGIVING

As the basis for this doorpiece, use a brown serving basket similar to the one shown. Bunch a generous quantity of floral clay at the lower rim of the basket to serve as a holder. In this, secure natural-colored wheat and small yellow and green gourds. (To make the gourds easier to handle, punch holes in the ends to accommodate sticks.) All these materials should be wired together. (Brown tape makes an effective cover for wires and sticks used in securing the material.) In the lower part of the basket, mingle small straw flowers in shades of yellow and brown with artificial carrots and peppers. Two feathered turkeys, one at the top and the other at the bottom of the design, contribute to the overall effectiveness of the doorpiece.

THANKSGIVING

Capture the colors of Thanksgiving by duplicating this crisp and original arrangement for your luncheon table. Begin with a basket container . . . the one here is an antique wire egg basket, but another type could be used just as effectively. Then push shrubbery sticks into the ends of corn, peppers, and lemons to facilitate arranging them. Leaving the tops on the corn, next place ears of corn, peppers and lemons in a balanced pattern as shown, using bunches of grapes at the handle of the basket and at the base. These may be secured in both places by using very fine wire. For depth and an added touch of color, place a few ivy leaves at the bottom of the arrangement.

THANKSGIVING

Not the usual Thanksgiving centerpiece, but the feeling is there, as you light the brown candle in the old amber lamp base. Color and depth are achieved here through imaginative placement of quite ordinary materials. First, wedge a tall, brown candle onto the rim of the lamp base and then arrange white button mums and Japanese grass low enough so that the candle may be lighted safely. Wire together varnished nuts and pine cones, and place them in the center of the container, allowing them to fall gently toward the base.

St. Valentine's Day

WHEN FEBRUARY fourteenth rolls around, great will be the excitement in the pigtail crowd . . . and a Valentine party given by Mommie will make the day sweet for everyone. For the invitations, send six-inch hearts cut out of red drawing paper. First divide each heart into two jagged pieces. Each youngster will then bring his "Broken Heart" to the party to find his secret pal. The guests will enjoy fitting the edges to find the matching half. Perfect fare for such an occasion are these pink-and-red Valentine Jamwiches. They're heart-shaped cookies, gaily iced and filled with raspberry jam. Serve them with ice cream. Of course, where children are, their mothers are not far behind. Serve the ladies pink-iced heart cookies . . . without the jam . . . and fragrant coffee.

Valentine Jamwiches

½ cup shortening	1 tablespoon vanilla
1 cup sugar	3½ cups sifted cake flour
2 eggs, well beaten	2 teaspoons baking powder
2 tablespoons light cream	½ teaspoon salt

Cream shortening and sugar together. Beat until light and fluffy. Add eggs, cream and vanilla and beat well. Mix and sift flour, baking powder and salt. Add to first mixture and mix well. Wrap in waxed paper or foil and chill. On board lightly dusted with confectioners' sugar, roll out dough about ¼ inch thick. Use large heart shaped cutter to cut dough into cookies. Use small heart shaped cutter to cut out centers of half the cookies, to make heart outlines. Dip cutter in confectioners' sugar each time before cutting cookie. Place cookies on lightly greased baking sheet. Bake in moderate oven, 375°F., for 8 to 10 minutes or until delicately browned. Cool. Frost heart outlines with pink icing. Spread whole large hearts with raspberry jam. Place iced outlines on jam-topped cookies, sandwich fashion. Makes about 30 large double cookies. The smaller hearts, made from cutting outlines, may be frosted with pink icing and served plain.

ST. VALENTINE'S DAY

To create this effective and romantic design for Valentine's day, use a figure in white alabaster as your starting point. A figure similar to the one shown here will do as well, but the white is important. To heighten the effect, place your white figure on a plain black stand, a little toward the back. Behind the figure, place a dish of water with a needle holder. Then spray yew branches with white paint to harmonize with the accessory and arrange them in a graceful line around the figure. Fill, with small hearts, the jar held by the figure, and fasten larger hearts on the yew branches in a balanced manner.

ST. VALENTINE'S DAY

To make this intriguing centerpiece for your St. Valentine's Day cocktail table, use floral clay to secure two milk glass, heart-shaped plates to a simple white base. Add a touch of red velvet ribbon, woven through the lattice edging of the plates, and your stage is set. Next, arrange red carnations and huckleberry foliage as shown, entwining small red hearts amid the foliage. Next, lay a larger red heart on the base . . . and scatter still more of the large red hearts around the table to be used as coasters for your cocktail glasses. For balance and ultimate contrast, place the finished arrangement on a red circular mat.

ST. VALENTINE'S DAY

Here's an old-fashioned valentine to appeal to the most romantic of tastes. To make this unique arrangement for your hall table or tea table, begin with an old glass lamp base. Use a large lump of floral clay in the top opening of the base to secure the arrangement. Construct both hearts by taking the metal from furnace filters, rolling them up tight, and shaping them into hearts. Then, wind thin red cord in and out around the hearts to make them more dominant. Now, arrange red and white carnations . . . with fresh greens . . . in a straight line, and place them in a needle cup holder behind the lamp base. Then, wire blue juniper tips together in the shape of another heart, and set the lamp base inside the heart-shaped juniper.

ST. VALENTINE'S DAY

An overall impression of graceful lines and delicate charm is accomplished with this design which you may create especially for St. Valentine's Day. Using a milk glass container, arrange white snapdragons so that each point stands out clearly. Use white carnations of varying stem lengths as your focal point, and intersperse brilliant red hearts in a balanced manner for contrast. The two milk glass, heart-shaped plates . . . with red velvet ribbon woven through the latticed edges . . . add color and balance to the arrangement.

Football Season

HAPPY DAYS are here again! With wonderful nippy weather, glorious Autumn colors and exciting activities, what's more thrilling than spending a Saturday afternoon at the football game? And, after the game is over, what's more fun than having your friends in for a buffet supper?

Decorate your table with colorful football symbols and traditional chrysanthemums. Prepare part of the food and set your buffet table in the morning. Then, when you and your friends arrive home from the game, rosy-cheeked and famished, serve food for hearty appetites.

MENU

Italian Spaghetti and Meat Balls

Tossed Green Salad

Garlic-toasted French Bread

Tea Cakes and Cookies

Coffee

Perry Como's
Old Country Italian Spaghetti Sauce

For each serving, combine:

one clove garlic, crushed	pinch of Oregano
1 teaspoon sugar	pinch of Basil
1 teaspoon salt	1 tablespoon pure olive oil

Fry in heavy iron skillet until garlic is almost brown. Add, for each serving, ¾ cup tomato paste and 1 cup water. Simmer over very low flame for half an hour.

FOOTBALL SEASON

You can delight your football enthusiasts at a buffet supper after the big game with this colorful arrangement for the refreshment table. First, select a low and fairly large container (the one used here is a bamboo scroll-type stand which has been turned upside down). To achieve the dominant colors, use yellow daisy mums and orange-colored marigolds . . . cutting the stems to various lengths and arranging them in a horizontal pattern as shown. For added interest and balance, place Korean barberry branches and sea oats (sprayed copper) toward the middle of your flower arrangement. Finally, add a few pine cones for transition from flowers to base, and two small footballs.

FOOTBALL SEASON

Win or lose, this unique table arrangement will delight your guests before or after the game. Begin with a genuine football helmet as the container. Make one arrangement of white mums and mahonia foliage inside the helmet. Then, in a cup holder behind the helmet, arrange more mums and mahonia foliage, as shown, so that they draw the eye toward the miniature goal posts. The goal posts add a note of originality to the arrangement, and are not hard to make. Construct them of heavy wire or of plywood; wrap in red ribbon, and top them with small streamers. Colors here, of course, are optional. You'll want to use the school colors of main interest to you and your guests.

Bird Supper

DID YOU ever watch a man at a bird supper? When the platter of birds is finally placed on the table, the men eye it with the fondness that only a hunter could understand. And that's one reason why the planning and preparation of the food and decorations . . . at this supper above all others . . . should be given extreme loving care. Too, they should follow the theme. I have used the Rock Cornish Game Hen in the menu below, but it is intended that you use whatever game your hunter has provided for you instead of the hen. The recipe for the wild rice and brandied peaches is from Patricia Murphy's book, *Glow of Candlelight.*

MENU
Relish Tray
Rock Cornish Game Hen or Other Bird
Caesar Salad
Cup Cakes
Coffee

Rock Cornish Game Hens with Wild Rice Stuffing and Brandied Peaches

4 Rock Cornish Game Hens	2 tablespoons minced celery
½ cup wild rice	1 tablespoon brandy
2 tablespoons pistachio nuts	Salt and pepper to taste
2 tablespoons melted butter	4 strips bacon
3 cooked pork sausages, chopped	½ cup water
1 tablespoon minced onion	2 tablespoons lemon juice

Wash birds; pat dry. Rub cavities with lemon juice and a little salt. Cook wild rice according to package directions; add nuts, melted butter, sausage, onion, celery, brandy, salt and pepper. Stuff birds with wild rice mixture. Truss. Criss cross half-strips of bacon over each bird. Place in a shallow baking pan large enough so that birds do not touch each other. Pour water and lemon juice into pan. Roast at 500° 15 minutes. Lower heat to 350°. Roast 45 minutes longer or until done. Baste with additional melted butter during last 15 minutes. Serve garnished with Brandied Peaches.* Makes 4 servings.

*Brandied Peaches

8 large canned cling peach halves	¼ cup dark brown sugar
¼ cup butter	3 tablespoons brandy

Saute peach halves gently in butter and sugar until lightly browned. Add brandy; simmer 5 minutes.

BIRD SUPPER

Simplicity is the keynote of this arrangement, designed for a table piece at a hunting party . . . or a duck dinner during the hunting season. On an alabaster mat (the one used here is green with a mottled effect) place seven rex begonia leaves in a large cup holder of water. Use a rock, preferably an interestingly shaped pink one, to add color and to conceal the cup holder. The alert mallard highlights the colors in the other materials and increases the effectiveness of the overall design.

BIRD SUPPER

Birds poised for flight recall the hunt . . . and this delicately beautiful design is perfect for a desk, table or mantel during the hunting season or at a bird supper. The lovely, polished burl base shown here is ideal for an arrangement of this type, but any wooden base may be used just as effectively. On your base, place a brass, footed stand to hold one bird figure, while the other figure is used below to achieve good balance. Spray juniper branches lightly with gold, and arrange them around the bird figures as shown. The figures here are bookends, but bird plaques or other ceramic birds could be used. To complete your arrangement, spray hen-and-chicks with gold paint and place on base.

BIRD SUPPER

This realistic design will be effective as a buffet supper table display
when you invite your friends in to enjoy the prizes of the hunt. To
create it for your table, begin with a delicately curved natural piece of
wood as your container. Then place fungus swirls on the wood piece as
shown, using a cup of water behind the fungus to hold your other materials . . . spikes of fresh bronze field dock and ferns. Arrange these
in a realistic manner with the dock as the center of interest. To firmly
establish your theme, use wild bird figures placed in realistic positions
on the piece of wood. The ones used here are made of brown feathers,
but ceramic figures of similar colors would also be effective.

BIRD SUPPER

The hunting season calls for informal breakfasts and parties galore, and this naturalistic design will make an attractive tablepiece for either occasion. A heavy piece of curved wood is your starting point in duplicating this arrangement. Fasten it to a block of wood with a screw and place it on a plaque (the one shown here is a polished burl). Next, fasten yew tips at the top and bottom of the piece of wood, using floral clay at the top and a cup holder at the base. Then bunch wired nuts together at top and bottom, letting them follow the curve of the wood. The ceramic squirrel used in the illustration is an appropriate accessory, but other types of wild life could be used as well.

Halloween

HALLOWEEN is everyone's pleasure . . . kids and parents alike. All you need to have fun on Halloween are a few yards of imagination and a room big enough and sturdy enough to accommodate a hungry gang of spooks. I suggest grilled hamburger roll-ups as the dish most likely to succeed. It's simply a new version of that old favorite, the hamburger, with all its best features built in. Have hot chocolate or cokes for the kids . . . plenty of hot coffee for the adults.

Stuffed Hamburger Roll-ups

2 lbs. ground beef	Soy sauce
1 cup cornflakes	¼ lb. American cheese
1 large tomato	1 dill pickle
½ cup barbecue sauce	10 frankfurter rolls

Salt and pepper

Season ground beef with salt and pepper and add cup of cornflakes. Then, dice the tomato and mix in, together with a half cup of your favorite barbecue sauce. Divide into 10 equal portions and pat each portion into thin, oblong patty. And here's the trick: marinate in soy sauce for twenty minutes. Cut cheese into 10 "sticks"; cut pickle into 10 strips. Place one cheese stick and one pickle strip on each patty. Roll up and grill over hot charcoal until cheese melts and meat is cooked. Serve in toasted frankfurter rolls. Makes 10 servings.

HALLOWEEN PARTY

This arrangement is the perfect conversation piece for your informal Halloween party, and it can be made in a matter of minutes. First, make a fence of three small pieces of wood nailed together, and secure it to a bamboo mat. Fill a rustic container with gourds and corn, adding corn tops at the corner as shown. Now add more gourds and corn at the base for transition and balance. The perky velvet cat and the colorful masks add interest . . . and provide additional emphasis.

HALLOWEEN PARTY

Here's something different for that Halloween party table. First, take a child's broom, and shorten the handle. Then, fasten it to a heavy burl plaque . . . angling it, as shown. Now, arrange tips of juniper and rhododendron in a cup of water . . . allowing the green to follow the line of the broom. Tuck in clusters of high bush cranberries and polished red apples on sticks. Then place three apples on the base, and a large, glass brandy snifter . . . half filled with water and apples.

HALLOWEEN PARTY

Here's a Halloween centerpiece that'll really delight your "trick or treaters." On your refreshment table, place first one large pumpkin with the traditional cut-out face and lighted candle inside. A small tray will make a perfect base for the pumpkin. Make a "hat" of gourds, straw flowers, corn tops, and bittersweet berries wired together and placed at the top opening of the pumpkin. Arrange oak leaves and small red apples on the tray around the pumpkin for added eye interest and balance. The black cat shown here is pinned on the wall directly behind the arrangement, and emphasizes the theme.

Children's Party

CHILDREN don't have to burst balloons to get a bang out of a party, but it helps. Because juvenile spirits are bound to run high at party time, you should be prepared to grin and bear it. But you'll have less to bear if you remove all breakables from the party area. A wonderful game for the four-to-six-year-olds is the "fishing game": Set enticing little packages on one side of a fire screen and have the guests "fish" for prizes with rod, line and safety pin. Nine-to-twelve-year-olds enjoy a "cook-it-yourself" party. But be sure to plan this step by step, showing the would-be chefs how to handle utensils and assigning each to his special job. For an unusual party cake, ice a round cake with pink icing and stud with fresh popcorn. Serve with ice cream.

Chocolate Cake

3 squares unsweetened chocolate	¼ cup Crisco
	1 cup sugar
1⅓ cups sifted cake flour	1 egg
1 teaspoon baking soda	1 cup milk
1 teaspoon salt	1 teaspoon vanilla

Start heating oven to 350°F. Line bottom of round pan (8″ in diameter) with waxed paper. Melt chocolate. Combine flour, soda and salt. Cream Crisco and sugar until light and fluffy; add egg and blend thoroughly. Blend in chocolate. Add flour mixture alternately with milk and vanilla. Pour into pan. Bake 50 minutes, or until cake tests done. Cool 15 minutes, then remove from pan to finish cooling.

Creamy Pink Icing

2 tablespoons water	1 egg
4½ tablespoons granulated sugar	½ cup Crisco
2⅓ cups sifted confectioners' sugar	1 teaspoon vanilla

Boil water and granulated sugar together a few minutes. Mix confectioners' sugar and egg. Blend with syrup. Add Crisco and vanilla. Beat until creamy. Add red vegetable coloring until the icing turns a pretty pink. Frost cake and stud with fresh popcorn.

CHILD'S PARTY

Little guests will be all eyes if you use this imaginative centerpiece at your child's birthday party. The central ingredient here is a colorful toy drum with a red candle on top. To make the arrangement, secure the candle to the top of the drum with floral clay, and place a cup holder with water to one side of the candle. Next, arrange clustered red roses, leaves of the corn, and hosta plant as shown . . . low enough so that the candle can be lighted. Place a few white stones at the base to conceal the cup holder, and add whirligigs as accessories.

CHILD'S PARTY

This delicate design for little people will make eyes bright at a child's birthday party. To make it, first fasten a plastic fence to a plain board plaque, using floral clay. Then, using two small cup holders, arrange boxwood branches as shown . . . high at the left and balanced by a lower arrangement at the right. A small boy or girl figure adds credence to the design . . . while the lollipops and candy kisses add a touch of sweetness. Each child should be given a lollipop to take home.

CHILD'S PARTY

The school crowd will be fascinated with this interesting arrangement of weeping leucothoe, red geraniums, wheat, and clusters of small tomatoes. To charm many a grade student, make this design for your refreshment table at your next party. Begin with a smooth board plaque and a rustic container. Arrange the leucothoe, geraniums, and other materials casually . . . letting tomatoes droop toward the base. Group bright red apples at the base . . . using slate and pencils as accessories to heighten the effect and add interest.

Graduation

GRADUATION should be one of the most serious, sentimental, and beautiful remembrances of a boy or girl's entire life. In planning a party for the occasion, keep your decorations simple and your refreshments easy for young, inexperienced party-goers to handle. In this way, there'll be fewer embarrassing faux pas. Make your young guests feel at ease and they'll shine their brightest. If they feel strained and shy, the party won't have the warm, glowing fellowship that the occasion deserves.

AFTERNOON TEA

Roquefort Dip with Crackers

Assorted Tea Sandwiches

Cup Cakes with Colored Frosting

Spiced Tea or Punch

Roquefort Dip

2½ oz. Roquefort cheese	1 teaspoon onion juice
8 oz. creamed cottage cheese	6 tablespoons sour cream

Crumble Roquefort cheese with fork and add to cottage cheese, mixing well. Stir in onion juice. Add sour cream, one tablespoon at a time, until mixture is of good dipping consistency. Serve with chips, crackers, or crisp raw vegetables. (You may tell your guests that this roquefort dip is Efrem Zimbalist, Jr.'s favorite recipe.)

GRADUATION OR DEBUTANTE PARTY

This permanent arrangement, symbolic of youth on the threshold, is perfect for the young girl graduate's room. Begin with a simple, modern vase and wedge styrofoam into the opening to hold the flowers. The ones used here are artificial . . . branches of flowering plum and pink roses (partially opened). Point one plum branch upward . . . the other downward in a graceful curve. The roses in the center of the branches draw the eye and become the focal point. The figure here seems to be looking toward the future and is a perfect accessory.

GRADUATION OR DEBUTANTE PARTY

Here's a tea-table decoration with a romantic appeal. There are no hearts, but plenty of fluff, and flowers. An iron, plant stand, with four holders for plants, is the container for pink and white carnations, purple statice, and arborvitae. In each holder of the stand, place a small needle cup holder full of water. Then group the plant material in each cup to form a well-balanced pattern . . . leaving the stand showing as a part of the overall picture. A purple cloth heightens the color harmony of the design . . . while white napkins, milk glass dishes, and candy in delicate colors add the finishing touches.

GRADUATION OR DEBUTANTE PARTY

Put a light in your girl graduate's eyes by duplicating this sparkling composition of roses and glass. Pretty perfume bottles are the ideal containers to use, but any other attractive bottles would be just as effective. Fill the bottles with water, strip the roses of most of their foliage, and arrange them in a simple manner, as shown. (The roses used here are the Margo Koster Polyantha rose, but any small ones would go well here.) Encircle the roses with variegated honeysuckle, and add a few red leaves of the Japanese maple to enhance the center. Now place one bottle high on a stand, and lay the bottle stoppers under the arrangement to reflect the rose color in the mirror base.

Easter

SPRING brings robins, flowers . . . and, best of all, Easter. Besides being a time of quiet dignity and regal lily arrangements, Easter is also a time for children. Chocolate bunnies, chicks, pretty new clothes, Easter baskets and egg hunts are all eagerly anticipated by the younger set. For entertainment, I would suggest an after-church brunch . . . including an outdoor egg hunt for the kids, complete with take-home decorations in the form of tiny Easter baskets (see pages 85 and 87). The recipe for Chicken Victor with Dumplings is from Patricia Murphy's book, *Glow of Candlelight*. This recipe could also be used for a buffet supper or dinner . . . in which case the menu could be Consomme, Chicken Victor with Dumplings, Escarole Salad, Layer Cake, and Coffee.

MENU for a BRUNCH
Fruit Cup
Country Ham on Tiny Biscuits
Chicken Victor with Dumplings
Scrambled Eggs
Sweet Rolls
Coffee

Chicken Victor with Dumplings

1 roasting chicken (3½ lbs.), disjointed	2 teaspoons baking powder
4 cups water	½ teaspoon sugar
1 small onion, chopped	½ teaspoon salt
2 stalks celery, sliced	2 tablespoons butter
1 teaspoon salt	1 egg, well beaten
⅛ teaspoon pepper	⅓ cup milk
1 cup sifted enriched flour	¼ pound snow peas, cooked
	1 can water chestnuts, sliced
	1 tablespoon lemon juice

Put chicken in kettle with water, onion, celery, salt and pepper. Bring to boil; simmer 45 minutes. Remove chicken; strain broth. Skin chicken; return to strained broth. Bring to boil. Meanwhile, mix and sift flour, baking powder, sugar and salt; cut in butter. Combine egg and milk; add to flour mixture; mix with a fork to soft dough. Drop by small spoonfuls into kettle, letting dough rest on pieces of chicken. Cook 10 minutes, uncovered; cover; cook 10 minutes longer. Remove dumplings and chicken to hot platter; keep warm. Thicken broth, if desired. Combine hot snow peas and sliced water chestnuts; add to platter. Pour some of the gravy over chicken. Serve remaining gravy separately. Serves four.

EASTER

Modern in design . . . yet with a touch of the old-fashioned . . . is this unusual arrangement for the Easter brunch table. A bamboo mat makes a good starting point for this composition. First, hold a palm leaf basket upright by using one heavy needle point holder in the front and one placed close in the back. Then arrange palmetto leaves as shown . . . in both the back and the front of the basket. Fashion a "nest" of pieces of palm and statice, and fill each nest with hand-colored eggs. The ones shown here have quaint Mexican designs on them for added color and interest. The perky hen balances the entire arrangement.

80

PALM SUNDAY

Here is an inspirational doorpiece in the modern motif for Palm Sunday. The design is startling in its beauty and simplicity, yet is relatively easy to make. First, take long palm branches, spray them lightly with gold paint, and wire them together as shown. Then make a swirl with sea grape leaves, which also have been sprayed with gold. Wire these quite low on the palm branches. Then for extra brightness, wire into the arrangement several foil "flowers" with variously colored centers. The "flowers" used here are silver with pink, purple, and green centers.

PALM SUNDAY

This dignified and cathedral-like design is perfect as an arrangement
for Palm Sunday. To make it, balance two wire candle holders on an
oval, black plaque. The candle holders used here produce the effect of
cathedral windows, but other holders could be used just as effectively.
Sprays of fresh palm should then be sprayed lightly with silver paint to
give a soft glow. Arrange these, as shown, in an upward movement, and
add the figure of the Madonna to contribute to the spirit of the design.

PALM SUNDAY

Warmth and new hope are the feelings imparted by this lovely design for Palm Sunday. The total effect is accomplished by a skillful handling of slender leaves of yellow and green palm. Arrange them so that the longer ones reach upward, and the others turn gracefully downward toward the lighted candle. Fashion a ribbon-like bow for the base from a few leaves of sansevieria and corn plant. Then clip a ceramic bird to the edge of the brass trivet holder for balance and added interest. The bird used here is in yellow to harmonize with the design.

EASTER

This Easter bonnet centerpiece will produce smiles from the family at Easter breakfast. Use a plain straw hat, with a yellow and brown bow, as a starting point for this design. Arrange yellow daisies and purple statice around the crown of the hat, and use a cup holder with water at the back to hold the upright arrangement of daisies and statice. Let the taller daisies lean gracefully over the crown of the hat, as shown. The three egg candles are optional, but they add a festive note.

EASTER

Tiny baskets, overflowing with flowers, form the basis for this unusual
Easter table centerpiece. To duplicate this unique design for your own
Easter table, place a shallow brass bowl on a cut bamboo mat. Next,
fasten a heavy curved branch inside the bowl with floral clay and hang
tiny baskets from top to bottom as shown . . . allowing one to rest on its
side on the base. In each little basket, arrange tips from white snapdragons, light and dark purple statice, and leather leaf fern tips. If you
will wrap the stems of each little arrangement in wet cotton and then
cover them with foil, the flowers will last for at least two days.

EASTER

This simple, but striking, design is very easy to make. First, secure a manzanita branch to a wooden plaque base by using floral clay. Then arrange yellow daffodils and purple heather around the branch, as shown . . . leaving the uppermost twigs bare. Add depth to the arrangement by placing a few pothos leaves among the daffodils and heather. Now, break a few colored eggs to resemble flowers, and scatter them casually at the base as shown. The eggs should harmonize in color.

EASTER

Bring a smile to little folks' faces this Easter with this novelty design
for a children's breakfast or luncheon. First, on a round woven mat
place a novelty chicken, similar to the one used here. In a cup holder,
toward the back of the mat, place branches of rhododendron. This will
make a nice background for the baskets. Now tie colorful bows lightly
around the top and center rhododendron leaf clusters, and hang tiny
baskets partially filled with candy Easter eggs. Arrange two or three
more baskets on the woven mat, with small eggs inside and out for
added eye interest. Lastly, place a little chick on either side.

EASTER

This intriguing design is short-lived because of the materials involved, but it gives a lot of pleasure while it lasts. To make it, first place a piece of driftwood in horizontal fashion on a green plastic mat. Set a brass stand with needle point holder behind the wood, and arrange Romaine lettuce, beans, carrots, and yucca leaves as shown. Place one bunny figure on the brass stand, which is partially concealed by the materials. Then arrange bib lettuce on the wood and at the base, and place the other bunny on the mat . . . as if about to nibble the lettuce. If you will soak the lettuce in ice water for several hours before you make this arrangement and then drain it, it will last several hours.

EASTER

Composed of simple materials, this natural scene is a perfect centerpiece for the Easter brunch table. The secret here is placement. Using a flat, grey-blue container with a needle point holder, arrange fluffy French pussy willows, flowing from left to right over the bowl. Be sure that each branch appears separate and individual. Next, place rounds of natural grey moss low among the pussy willows, and a large grey rock to conceal the holder. Place ceramic rabbits, one grey and one brown, as shown, to complete the effect.

EASTER

Here's an arrangement in candy and fern to delight the children at Easter. Focal point of the easy-to-make and attractive design is a large chocolate rabbit sporting a colorful bow. The container here is a brown, flat bowl which has been turned upside down, but you may wish to use a variation of this. Secure the back material . . . brown Japanese grass, natural and sparkled cattails . . . with floral clay. Make nests of air fern, and add candy eggs wrapped in colored foil.

EASTER

Reflecting the spiritual significance of Easter, this quiet and beautiful arrangement will be a real inspiration . . . no matter where you place it. Begin with a delicately carved plaque placed flat as a base. Then secure the cup holder off-center and slightly toward the back of the plaque. Several Easter lilies with stems of varying lengths are used for height, and the mass of blooms at the base conceals the holder. Florist wire is taped to the stems for necessary strength. To add depth and freshness, corn plant leaves (dracena) and nephthytis are placed at the base, and a complementing ribbon marker has been placed in the open Bible. The slim white twisted candle in its glass candlestick adds an ethereal quality which heightens the spiritual appeal of this design.

EASTER

Simplicity spells drama in this striking design for Easter. On an alabaster base (turned upside down for a rougher surface), place first a large white rock, such as the one shown here, representing the stone which was rolled away from the tomb of Christ. Then spray three palm leaves with white paint, and secure them behind the rock. Lastly, place two alabaster angels, one on either side of the rock (kneeling at the tomb), to complete the arrangement.

St. Patrick's Day

THE FIRST RULE of successful party-giving is to always have a reason for your party . . . other than to fulfill social obligations. It can be a farewell party, a housewarming, bridal shower, or even getting together on St. Patrick's Day to smoke clay pipes or sing Irish songs. But have a reason. One of the most entertaining parties I've heard of was a Beatnik evening. The guests came dressed as Beatniks, and read poetry to jazz and tried to talk in Beatnik lingo. This is the sort of thing that makes people gay and festive. No matter how frivolous the reason, if you give a party with a purpose, it's much easier to make it fun. It provides a theme for the evening, a flavor to the conversation, and nudges people out of their shells. It gives a novelty twist to your decorations and your refreshments. For a St.Patrick's day celebration, try the following buffet menu to carry out the color scheme.

MENU

Congealed Lime Salad

Irish Beef Stew

Peppermint Puffs

Coffee

Peppermint Puffs

Make 6 large puffs according to directions on Betty Crocker Cream Puff Mix package, using one stick mix. Cool. Remove tops from puffs and fill (recipe below). Top each puff with a small dab of filling and a little crushed candy, if desired. Serve with Quick Chocolate Mint Sauce (recipe below).

Filling: Beat 2 cups whipping cream until stiff. Fold in 1 cup *finely* crushed green peppermint candy, and a few drops of green food coloring. This recipe makes enough for 6 large puffs.

Quick Chocolate Mint Sauce: Melt 6-oz. package semi-sweet chocolate pieces over hot water. Beat in 5½ oz. can evaporated milk and ⅛ teaspoon salt. Blend in ½ teaspoon peppermint extract (not oil of peppermint which is much stronger).

ST. PATRICK'S DAY

Irish or not, your guests will be intrigued with this luncheon table decoration for St. Patrick's Day. Artificial shamrocks and winged alatus branches are the only materials needed to make this attractive design. Using a candy dish as your container, place a small needle holder in it, and arrange winged alatus branches. To obtain the ultimate in color brilliance, spray the alatus with white paint. Then fasten the shamrocks to the branches with wire, arranging them so that they appear to be flowers . . . grouping some of them in the container as shown. Finally, place the container on a glass base to dramatize the white clay accessories and highlight the overall arrangement.

ST. PATRICK'S DAY

The "wearin' of the green" is highlighted in this coffee table design for St. Patrick's Day. To duplicate this unique arrangement, you need a hat (the one shown is glass, but a paper one would be effective), aspidistra leaves, and artificial shamrocks. First, place the hat in the center of a plain Irish linen mat. Then wire aspidistra leaves by placing the wire along the middle of the leaf in the back, and use Scotch tape to conceal the wire. The leaves can then be shaped in any curve you desire. Using a needle point holder or a lump of floral clay, place the leaves toward the back of the hat, as if they were trimming on it. A few shamrocks arranged at the base complete the design.

Christmas·

THE GALA SPIRIT of holiday family dinners makes them the most cherished occasions of a lifetime. And there's no finale more fitting or festive for a Christmas dinner than beautiful Café Brulôt Diabolique. The room is darkened . . . the only light is the flickering burner beneath the chafing dish. Then a match is held to the spiced cognac in the shallow dish, while hot demitasse coffee is slowly poured over blue flames. This is the glittering moment . . . yellow and blue flame leaps and swirls 'round the dark stream of coffee. Each face at the table lights up in a glow of pride and delight as they watch the festive magic. And, long after they have sipped the truly delicious brew, the glow continues to warm their hearts in real holiday fashion.

This particular recipe comes from famed Antoine's in New Orleans where the flambé creation is the specialité de la maison. Actually, it's so simple to make, it can always be your own family specialty.

Café Brulôt Diabolique

6 pieces of lump sugar	1 cut-up lemon peel
8 whole cloves	4 jiggers cognac brandy
1 one-inch cinnamon stick	1 quart hot demitasse coffee

Place all ingredients, except hot demitasse coffee, in chafing dish. Ignite cognac with match and stir ingredients until well blended. After a minute or two, slowly pour in the hot black coffee and continue to stir. (In winter, heat brandy before using.) Makes 4 generous servings. To serve, strain into *Brulôt* or demitasse cups.

CHRISTMAS

Friends who drop in at Christmas time will be enchanted with this attractive candle-tree arrangement. Use a brass candle-tree as the framework for your design. Then, using Scotch tape, fasten clusters of small fruits and green velvet bows to the tree, as shown. Use red candles as the finishing touch to this simple but striking arrangement.

CHRISTMAS

A delicate glass tree with its lid removed becomes the base for this colorful but dignified Christmas centerpiece. Fill each section of the tree with fresh crab apples, artificial holly leaves, and berries. In the top section of your tree, place a tall, red candle. Tape foliage and artificial fruits part of the way to the top, as shown. Harmonizing fruits and foliage are placed at the bottom of the tree for balance.

CHRISTMAS

This winter wonderland on your Christmas refreshment table will captivate all of your guests, large and small. Place a large urn-type white container on a styrofoam base. Secure a heavy manzanita branch to the urn with floral clay, and arrange snow-sprayed branches of Scotch pine, as shown, fastening them into the clay. Place one snowman on the base, and two snowballs of styrofoam amid the lower pine branches. The other snowman should be perched gaily in the center of the container. Wedge more snowballs of varying sizes onto the twigs of the manzanita branch, and your winter scene is complete.

CHRISTMAS

This design, representing perfection in pastels, will surely attract attention at Christmas time. And the unusual effect here is obtained with a minimum of materials and time. Using a silver meat tray or other serving tray as a base, group candles graduated in size and in varying hues of orchid as shown here. Then arrange, in a flower-like manner, orchid glass Christmas trims, artificial fruits, and some gold foil leaves to harmonize and balance with the candles. Although greens are not necessary, some fresh greens could be used if desired.

CHRISTMAS

This wispy, ethereal design departs from the traditional red and green
of Christmas, perfectly depicting the adoration theme in very soft
shades of gold. To create it, begin with two curving branches of
euonymus which have been sprayed lightly with gold paint. Entwine
these to form a circle, using a cup holder to hold them at the bottom.
Within the circle and slightly toward the back, place twin gold
candle holders to give elevation to the angels and the illusion of motion. Two of the angel figures should be fastened to the holders with
floral clay, while the third angel and the Christ Child are placed on a
stand in front of the circle to give balance.

CHRISTMAS

As intricate and intriguing as this wall arrangement looks, it is not too difficult to compose. First, select a basket planter similar to the one shown here, and spray it lightly with gold paint. Then fill it with a colorful grouping of luminous fruits, glitter grapes, and glass sprays, holding the material in place with floral clay and wire. The small angel plaques are placed on the wall, and their apparent hovering about the basket adds interest and balance to the design.

CHRISTMAS

The delicate, rather fragile quality of this arrangement makes it a perfect one for the center of your light refreshment table at Christmas. To make it, fasten a white coral spray with floral clay on the top of a tall, white vase. Arrange artificial pine branches as shown . . . one at the back, one through the center, and one brought well down. In the midst of the pine branches, place green, gold, and red Christmas tree balls. Now place two silvered sea fans on a red or green cloth, and set the vase on this base. Lastly, round out your centerpiece by scattering various Christmas trims at the base, to give unity.

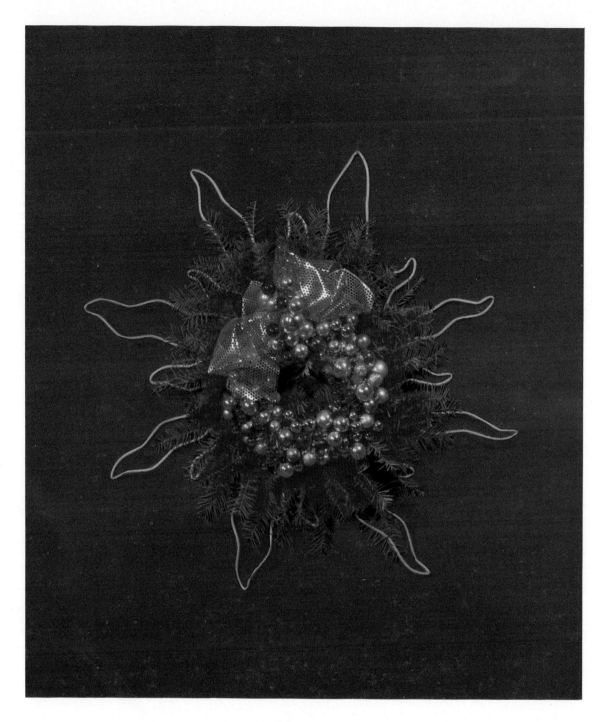

CHRISTMAS

Here is a clever way to use your broken Christmas tree balls and make an elegant door decoration for Christmas. To make it, first form your sunburst pattern as shown . . . using heavy reed, wire, or some other pliable material. Next, spray the sun burst with silver paint. To make the wreath, which is the center of interest, use a low-cost wreath, pour glue around and through it, and secure broken Christmas balls in it until the entire surface is covered, as shown. Add a bow of silver metallic cloth and a few tips of yew to give your design a fresh look.

CHRISTMAS

The artistic employment of a minimum of materials results in this delicate and beautiful doorpiece for the Christmas season. To make it for your own front door, begin with a strong manzanita branch as your base. Next, wire tips of Scotch pine to the manzanita in a realistic manner, following the curve of the branch. Here and there, keeping in mind depth and balance, wire feathered red birds. Lastly, add a large, red satin bow at the bottom, and your simple but eye-catching door-piece will be ready to welcome friends all through the season.

CHRISTMAS

Simple, yet lovely in composition, this design will bring a bit of the forest into your home at Christmas. Using polished wood as your base, first fashion a little yew tree by taking a small bamboo stick and wedging it into a cone of styrofoam. Cover the foam with three-inch tips of yew until no white is visible. Then spray the tree lightly with gold paint and trim it with natural cones. Secure it firmly to the base with floral clay, scattering cones at the base to conceal the clay. The piece of driftwood with carved buck and doe at either end provides added interest and completes the rustic theme.

CHRISTMAS

Elegant for either Thanksgiving or Christmas, this arrangement is a symphony in rich tones of brown, green, and gold. The overall effect is achieved here by skillful placement of only three materials . . . small, decorative pineapples, palmetto leaves, and varnished pecans. First, wedge sticks into the ends of the pineapples to make them pliable, spray lightly with gold paint, and arrange in a heavy modern green and gold compote. Behind the pineapples, secure palmetto leaves, which have also been sprayed with gold paint. Then drape clusters of varnished pecans as shown, allowing them to spill over the compote at the bottom. This arrangement is best suited for heavy furniture . . . with heavy mats and other accessories to harmonize.

CHRISTMAS

Perfect for that gay, informal Christmas breakfast is this study in symmetry. Using white milk glass containers (dinner goblets are shown here), wedge enough styrofoam into each to hold red candles and other materials securely. Next, place one piece of artificial fern toward the back of your arrangement and another toward the front of each container, being careful to maintain balance. Then arrange a quantity of small apples and strawberries on heavy wire and insert one "string" of them into each container as shown . . . striving for identicalness. Lastly, add a small bowl of real strawberries and apples for balance.

Colonial Candle Co

HYANNIS, MA

SPECIAL O

For use only when your dealer cann

trated in our Booklet entitled "Decor

To: Colonial Candle Co., of Cape Co
Hyannis, Massachusetts

Gentlemen:

Please send me the following c

QUANTITY	NAME OF CAND

Check or Money Order

for $............................ enclosed

MY LOCAL DEALER'S NAME AND AD

....

Signed (Please print) ....

Street and Number or RFD ....

City or Town ....

CHRISTMAS

A blend of the traditional and the modern produces this beautifully balanced centerpiece for your Christmas entertaining. Begin with a mirror base, a tall, green glass compote, and two green glass bubbles. In a cup holder placed toward the back of the container, arrange an airy spray of carnations with mahonia foliage for added weight and interest. The green glassware and leaf dish give solidity and balance to your arrangement . . . and the silken cord around the edges of the mirror highlights the red of the carnations and serves to frame the mirrored reflection. A red Christmas candle inside the globe gives a faint glow.

CHRISTMAS

The effect of graceful motion is conveyed in this Christmas arrangement, perfect for a small table in the guest room. An old brass angel candle holder is the basis of this design. To make it, form a ball from moderately heavy wire, and then wrap it in foil. Fasten it to the candlestick with floral clay. Make a bow of pink tinsel for the top of the ball, and group small pink glass grapes with silver leaves in the center.

CHRISTMAS

An old candle mold with slim, white, twisted candles give the impression of a pipe organ with choir boys. To create this unique arrangement, place the candle mold toward the back of a burl base. Next, stand slim, white twisted candles in the mold, as shown. Then arrange china choir boys in such a way that they will give balance and direct the eye toward the candles. Juniper tips at the left, top, and bottom soften and coordinate the separate parts.

CHRISTMAS

To please a child at Christmas, use a small sleigh with lots of toys and some kind of a Santa. Begin by putting a cup holder inside a gold sleigh . . . to keep the greens fresh . . . and arranging spruce branches as shown. Now hang tiny, gaily colored toys on the strong branches of the spruce. Provide a toy for each child to take home.

CHRISTMAS

This design will assure a touch of the dramatic at Christmas time almost anywhere you put it. Using an old lamp base, or similar container sprayed with silver paint, arrange common dried field dock in a tree shape as shown. Secure the branches in a large lump of floral clay. Spray the field dock heavily with silver paint, and for striking contrast, add tiny pink glitter grapes and pink tinsel. Dramatically displayed against a plain backdrop, your tree will attract attention.

CHRISTMAS

This tree form can be used in pairs on your mantel, or balanced with candles at the opposite end from it. First, make your tree form by cutting 1/4-inch hardware wire into the desired shape. Fasten the form to a dowel stick with tacks, and wedge styrofoam into the container to secure your tree. The container used here is a green compote-type vase, but a painted flower pot would also be an excellent choice. Cover the tree shape with dried hydrangea blossoms, dried Japanese grass, and a dried field weed painted white. Insert a few small Christmas balls for brightness, and spray the entire tree with copper paint. The brown and green satin bow adds color and interest.

CHRISTMAS

These trees, with their Oriental flair, are permanent and may be used from Christmas to Christmas with variations. To make them, whittle six pieces of wood as shown and then glue them together. Each tree should be secured in a block of wood, with a hole bored to accommodate the lower wood spoke. Trim each small tree with colorful glass beads and tiny birds or angels, as desired. If you wish, you may heighten the effect of your trees by spraying them with silver or gold.

CHRISTMAS

Gracefulness and simplicity make this Christmas scene entirely captivating. The brass trivet makes an effective base for this arrangement, which is composed of materials of green and gold. Using artificial fern as the mainstay of this design, combine beige sprayed gold grass, money plant, and artificial japonica foliage, letting the fern bend gently at the top, over the head of the Madonna. The hovering angels, also tinged with green and gold, add balance and interest.

CHRISTMAS

Cone wreaths are beautiful . . . and last forever. To make one, begin with a double florist wreath form and pine cones of average uniform size. Using firm wire, wire one row of cones in the center as shown and one row around the outer edge, leaving a small space between. To heighten the effect of your wreath, be sure that the row around the inner side skips every other space. Add richness by entwining green mahonia leaves among the cones in the outer ring and a gold metallic ribbon, trailing gracefully downward. The angel at the top right of the wreath adds eye interest.

CHRISTMAS

The charm of this contemporary design, perfect for a hall table at Christmas or the New Year, lies in its contrasting components . . . the rugged, angular branch and the satin-smooth doves in their tinsel nests. Begin with a simple white or alabaster compote and the branch, painted a shiny black. Fasten the branch in the center of the bowl with floral clay. Fashion dainty nests of tinsel, placing one high on the branch, the other in the compote. Arrange white doves or other similar birds in a downward sweep. For maximum effectiveness, place this design on a hall table. It will attract a lot of attention.

CHRISTMAS

This tree, made of teasels from the field, is easily constructed. Using a styrofoam cone for the base, place teasels lightly sprayed with silver paint all around the outer edge, leaving a space in between each one for airiness. To achieve depth without bulkiness, place every other pod in close, and the other toward the outside. Decorate your tree with colored balls (those shown here are a deep pink), and, of course, use your own favorite ornament at the top of your tree. The container is a wooden compote placed on a silver star. The additional pods placed on the star give the needed transition between mount and tree.

CHRISTMAS

The Eastern motif is evident in this simple but effective desert scene. A wooden bread board or burl makes an excellent base for this design, which would be attractive on your mantel at Christmas. To achieve this study in tones of brown and copper, first fasten a heavy needle point holder to the base with floral clay. Use sprigs of statice and grey moss with rocks at the bottom to stabilize the arrangement . . . and place cut palm leaves at the base of a palm plume. Work upward from this base, using more sprigs of statice, leading the eye to the star at the top, fashioned of two palm leaves wired together. Spray all of these materials lightly with copper paint. The carved camels, placed in a line to simulate motion, complete the scene.

CHRISTMAS

Bells and candles in gold and green are the basis for this traditional arrangement, perfect for a mantel at Christmas. Begin with gold bells, one a little larger than the other. (The ones used here are planter bells.) Place one bell high on a plant holder and the other one low and at a different angle, as shown. Behind the bells, place a twin candle holder to hold gold candles, and arrange gold-sprayed, blue-spruce branches between the bells and candles. Now add some gold balls and a few sprigs of pine inside the bells. You might wish to make another identical piece and use one at each end of your mantel . . . or just more bells and greens to finish out a mantel composition.

121

CHRISTMAS

This tree, made of wire, is a most fitting Christmas decoration in a very modern room. Form the tree with moderately heavy wire, being sure to leave two heavy wires at the bottom that will hold it upright in or on a styrofoam base. Wrap each "branch" of your tree with both silver and blue tinsel, add two modern angels, placed as shown, conceal the base at least partially with greens, and your decoration is complete. Hang it where it will be the focal point of interest.

122

CHRISTMAS

For a modern decor, basket trees are smart . . . and can very often be found in basket shops. Entwine silver tinsel around and around the tree. Then spray tree and tinsel with gold paint to give it a sparkling effect. Place small foil butterflies in gold and blue all around the tree. Then put the finished decoration on a gold woven mat, scattering more butterflies on the mat. The large butterfly shown here, which is a brass accessory, may be omitted.

CHRISTMAS

These bells will almost ring out a welcome to your Christmas-time guests as they come to your door. Yet, this lacy doorpiece is fashioned primarily from the metal panels from furnace filters! First, take one panel, and shape it into a large bell; then, cut another panel in half. From the halves, make two bells for the top of the piece. Wire these together as shown. Use three or four commercially made bells at the top and a string of small bells through the lower bell. Add a bow of silver metallic ribbon, and you'll have an attractive doorpiece that will last all through the holiday season. If you're going to use the bells on a white door, you may want to add some fresh greens.

CHRISTMAS

An antique stand is a perfect container for this richly colored assortment of fruits and ferns. Arrange dwarf, decorative pineapples, sprayed with gold paint, treated brown leather-leaf fern, and sprayed gold and red crab apples as shown. Impale the small red apples on toothpicks so that they will stay in place. Use red candles in gold candle holders to heighten the color scheme. Fruit plates reflecting the pattern of the arrangement and glass cups and saucers to catch the soft light of the candles are excellent with this design. The pineapple on the mat provides the transitional element, completing the arrangement.

CHRISTMAS

Serenity in an oval frame is the message of this quiet Madonna arrangement, perfect for some secluded spot in the home at Christmas. Begin with a silver frame, and fasten it securely to a block of wood. Place branches of silvered leucothoe in a graceful line, with green and white satin grapes and plastic gardenias sweeping downward to conceal the block and highlight your picture. Place a Madonna figure inside the frame (the figure here is of green and white porcelain). A silver candle holder with a lighted silver candle will give your picture soft illumination and provide balance.

126

CHRISTMAS

The candle and the wreath . . . in themselves symbols of the Christmas season . . . are used in a unique manner here to give a totally new effect. Make a wreath by using a double floral wreath frame and wiring pine cones, sprayed lightly with gold paint, to the inner and outer circles. As shown here, the wreath can be embellished by adding boxwood tips and gold flower Christmas trims. Place the wreath upright against a plain wall, with the aid of a heavy plate holder. A brandy snifter with candle inside should be placed on a brass stand so that it appears to be near the center of the wreath.

CHRISTMAS

Here's an effective and young-looking doorpiece that is easy to do. Simply take branches of blue spruce, or other greens, and wire them into a pattern. Spray them with plastic snow, and fasten a bow and a couple of favorite Christmas toys. The design here uses a red cord bow and streamer, with two red and green Pixies.